Snowboarding
in Action

John Crossingham

Illustrations by Bonna Rouse

Crabtree Publishing Company

www.crabtreebooks.com

Created by Bobbie Kalman

Dedicated by John Crossingham
For Greg Davis, for giving me the coolest job around

Editor-in-Chief
Bobbie Kalman

Author
John Crossingham

Project editor
Amanda Bishop

Editors
Niki Walker
Kathryn Smithyman

Copy editor
Jaimie Nathan

Cover and title page design
Campbell Creative Services

Computer design
Margaret Amy Reiach

Production coordinator
Heather Fitzpatrick

Photo researcher
Jaimie Nathan

Consultant
Lee Gregory Johnson
Olympic Halfpipe Judge, Nagano, Winter 1998

Photographs
Bruce Curtis: pages 8, 9, 12, 14 (top), 15, 16, 21, 25,
29 (top), 30
Photography by www.insight-photography.com:
pages 23, 26, 28
Other images by Adobe, Corbis Images,
PhotoDisc, and Digital Stock

Illustrations
All illustrations by Bonna Rouse except the following:
Margaret Amy Reiach: pages 9 (bottom), 30, 31

Crabtree Publishing Company

www.crabtreebooks.com   1-800-387-7650

PMB 16A
350 Fifth Avenue
Suite 3308
New York, NY
10118

612 Welland Avenue
St. Catharines
Ontario
Canada
L2M 5V6

73 Lime Walk
Headington
Oxford
OX3 7AD
United Kingdom

Cataloging-in-Publication Data
Crossingham, John
 Snowboarding in action / John Crossingham;
illustrations by Bonna Rouse.
    p. cm. -- (Sports in action)
Includes index.
This book describes the history of snowboarding, as well as
equipment, skills, competitions, and tips for good snowboarding.
  ISBN 0-7787-0125-5 (pbk.) -- ISBN 0-7787-0119-0 (RLB)
 1. Snowboarding--Juvenile literature. [1. Snowboarding.]
I. Rouse, Bonna, ill. II. Title. III. Series.
 GV857.S57 C76 2002
 796.9--dc21
                                                                LC 2002002275

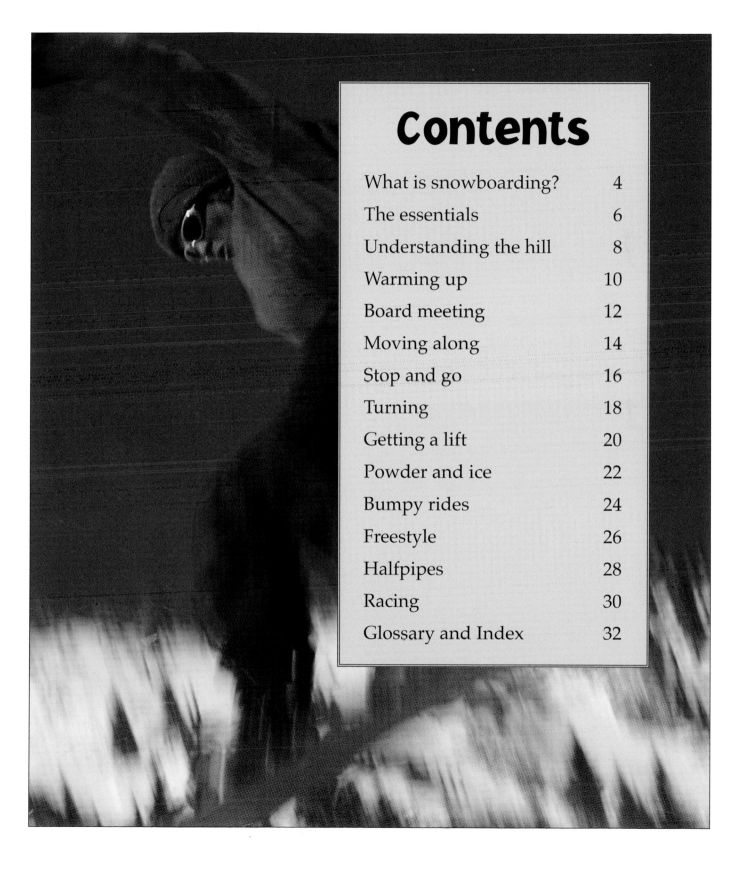

Contents

What is snowboarding?

Snowboarding is a winter sport that combines downhill skiing, surfing, and skateboarding. Snowboarders ride long boards down snow-covered mountains. Although people once thought it was a fad, the sport has become as popular as skiing. Most snowboarders do not compete in events. They simply enjoy riding down hills or challenging themselves by performing moves called **tricks**.

Competitive snowboarders can participate in a variety of events. In **freestyle** snowboarding competitions, boarders perform tricks. Judges give the tricks a score based on difficulty and originality. Snowboarders also compete in races on different types of **courses**. Snowboarding events such as racing and freestyle halfpipe competitions were added to the Winter Olympics in 1998.

Snowboarding through fresh snow is great exercise and a lot of fun.

The essentials

Snowboarding requires many accessories—a snowboard, a jacket, snowpants, boots, and gloves are just some of the items you will need. This equipment can be expensive, so if you are still growing, try to find it at local second-hand sports stores. Make sure that any equipment you buy fits you well and is in good condition.

Watch your head

When snowboarding, wear a tight-fitting hat to keep your head and ears warm. Goggles or, on bright days, sunglasses are also important. Both protect your eyes from wind, snow, and the sun's rays. Remember to use sun block and lip balm as well! It may not be hot, but on a sunny day your skin can burn quickly because snow reflects sunlight.

Snowsuit

Snowboarding jackets and pants come in many colors and styles. Choose whatever makes you feel most comfortable, but be sure your clothes are warm and waterproof—nothing is colder than a wet bottom in winter! Jackets or pants with extra pockets are helpful for carrying items. Finally, don't forget to wear long underwear and thick socks.

Helmets

If you are serious about snowboarding, buy a snowboarding helmet. A helmet can prevent serious injuries caused by a fall or an accident.

Buddy system

Always snowboard with a friend. If you become tired or get stuck in deep snow, your friend can find help for you.

The deck

The "board" of a snowboard is called the **deck**. Decks come in many sizes and styles. Each deck is made to suit a style of boarding as well as the boarder's height. The **base**, or bottom of the deck, is smooth and slides easily over the snow. The **rail**, or edge of the deck, is a thin strip of metal that helps you grip snow and ice as you board.

rail

base

*Snowboarders often talk about the **nose**, or front, of the board, and the **tail**, or back, of the board.*

Boots

Boots come in different styles to suit each boarder's needs. Soft boots look and feel like winter boots. They are good for freestyle and casual boarders who want comfort.

Hard boots are made of firm plastic shells. These boots allow boarders to control their boards easily. Racers use hard boots.

For a boarder who likes a bit of both styles, **hybrid** boots are also available.

Bindings

Bindings attach the boots to the deck. Highback bindings have straps that wrap around soft boots.

Plate bindings hold hard boots in place. These bindings firmly grip the front and rear of the boot.

Step-in bindings have notches that lock into the bottom of hybrid boots.

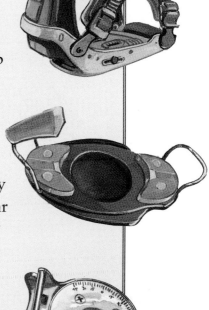

Understanding the hill

A ski hill is a lot of fun, but it can also be a dangerous place. Every resort has a set of rules that skiiers and boarders must follow. Before you hit the hill, learn the rules of the resort where you are boarding. Always be respectful and look out for other boarders and skiers. Nothing ruins a good time like an injury or being kicked off your favorite hill!

Smooth running

Ski hills are divided into separate courses called **runs**. Helpful signs are posted on the hill to guide you through each run and keep you out of trouble. Runs have names to help people remember them and use them as meeting places—for example, "We'll meet at the top of Snowflake at 1:30."

Safe lodging

Be sure to get a pocket-sized map of the whole hill before you start. At most resorts, maps are free. On your map, make a note of the runs you intend to do and the location of the **lodges**. These rest buildings have everything from food and restrooms to **ski patrol**, which is the hill's ambulance service. Smaller hills have only one lodge, but some resorts have several. Know where to go in case of an emergency.

Try to keep space between yourself and other people on the hill.

Read the signs

Some runs are more difficult than others. Ski hills all over the world use the same symbols to show the difficulty of each run.

Hills marked with a green circle are beginner hills. They have smooth, even slopes and no obstacles. Green runs are good places to learn to balance on your board or just warm up for the day. They are also known as "bunny hills."

Runs with a blue square are medium level or "more difficult" runs. These hills are a little steeper than bunny hills and may have obstacles such as **moguls**, or bumps. Use these runs to challenge yourself as you become familiar with your board.

Runs with a black diamond are the most difficult runs on the mountain. These exciting runs are steep, uneven, and often full of moguls. Some hills also have double-black-diamond runs, which are for experts only. Do not try these unless you are certain of your abilities, or you'll find yourself stranded and waiting for the ski patrol to rescue you!

Lift tickets

Lifts are machines that carry you up a ski hill. They are not free. To ride the lifts, you need a **lift ticket**. A lift ticket is a sticker that attaches to your jacket. Don't lose it—no ticket, no ride! You can buy full-day, half-day, and nighttime tickets. If you plan to ski every weekend, you can also buy a season's ticket.

Warming up

Snowboarding is a tough sport. Bouncing on the hill and flying down the mountain can wear down your back, legs, and neck. Before you head out on the hill, be sure to take a few minutes to stretch. Stretching can save you from getting a strained muscle or other injury.

Trunk circles

Put your hands on your hips and place your feet shoulder-width apart. Keep your feet flat on the ground as you swing your hips around in circles. Do three circles to the right and three to the left.

Leg crossovers

Stand and cross your legs at the ankles. Bend at the waist and slowly reach for your toes. Keep your knees slightly bent and stretch as far as you can do so comfortably. Hold the stretch for five seconds and then straighten up and switch legs. Stretch each leg five times.

Neck circles

It is easy to hurt your neck, so do this stretch carefully. Keep your chin tucked toward your chest and slowly roll your head from side to side. Never roll your head backward and only stretch as far as feels comfortable.

Quadriceps stretch

Stand on your left foot and use your left hand to support yourself against a wall. Lift your right foot behind you until you can grab it with your right hand. Pull gently until you feel the stretch in the front of your leg. Hold the stretch for a count of ten and then switch legs.

Ankle stretch

Sit on the ground with one leg straight. Bend your other leg so that you can grab your foot. Gently move it in circles. When you have done ten circles, do ten more in the other direction. Change legs!

Leg lunges

Spread your feet apart as far as you can. Lunge by bending one knee and keeping the other leg straight. You can rest your hands on your bent knee or on the ground. Count to five. Do five lunges on each side.

"V" Stretch

Sit with your legs in a "V." Stretch your arms out in front of you until you feel the pull in the back of your legs and buttocks. Hold the stretch for a count of ten.

Board meeting

Part of getting to know your snowboard is finding your **stance**. The stance is the position of your feet, legs, and upper body as you ride. Snowboarders stand sideways on their boards, as skateboarders do. If you skateboard, you already know which foot will be closer to the nose of the board. If not, imagine going up to bat in baseball. The foot nearest the pitcher is your front foot. For most people, the left foot is the front foot. This stance is called **regular**. For some people, however, the right foot is the front foot. This stance is called **goofy**. All the instruction in this book are for regular-stance snowboarders. If you ride goofy, change left to right in the instructions.

Attaching your bindings

Bindings are attached to your board after you buy the equipment. Once you figure out your stance, stand on the board to get your **stance angle**, or the angle at which your bindings will be attached to the board. Generally, your front foot will point more forward than your back foot.

Stepping on

How you attach your boots depends on the type of bindings you have (see page 6). Ask a ski shop employee or instructor how to attach your boots properly and practice attaching them at home. On the hill, always brush excess snow from the boots and bindings before you attach them. Don't forget to tie the **leash**, which is the strap that goes from the front binding to your ankle. If your bindings come loose, the leash will prevent the board from flying down the hill.

Staying centered

Good balance is a key to good snowboarding. If you lean forward and back with just your head and shoulders, you'll probably fall over. You have to learn to keep your weight **centered** over your board. You'll know that your weight is centered when you feel steady even while leaning back or forward. If you feel as though you may tip over, your weight isn't centered. Practice these balancing exercises on a patch of snow in your backyard or at a park.

1. Try to balance on your toe edge, or the rail of the board closest to your toes. Push your upper body forward but keep your shoulders balanced over the board. Your heels naturally rise, and you are balancing on your toes. You are weighting onto your toe edge and unweighting from your heel edge.

2. Now try balancing on your heel edge, or the rail closest to your heels. Push out your backside but keep your shoulders over the board. Now your toes rise, and you are resting on your heels. Hold the position for a few seconds and then bring your backside over the board again.

Pivoting

Pivoting is another helpful exercise that will help you get used to your board. Pivoting is used to steer down a hill. You can practice it in your backyard. Use your lower body (feet and legs) to turn your board from left to right. Imagine that the center of your board is attached to the ground—only the nose and tail move back and forth.

Use your back foot to do most of the pivoting. As you get better, try keeping your front foot almost still. Lean most of your weight on it to keep it in place.

Moving along

Once you start feeling comfortable on your board, try sliding and stopping. Do these moves on a flat surface. You do not even need to go up a ski hill. Any spot that is open and free of crowds is fine.

One foot at a time

You will slide to get from lodge to lodge and over flat areas. You also slide to move through **lift lines** (see page 20). To practice sliding, start on a flat surface with only your front foot in the binding. Use your back foot to push off the snow. This motion is similar to pushing a skateboard. After a few pushes, place your back foot on the **stomp pad** and glide in a straight line. Try not to stare at your feet. Keep your head up and look forward.

Edging

Most of the time that you are riding, you will be **edging**, or balancing on one rail. Rail edges dig into the snow and give you control. Once you feel comfortable sliding in a straight line, try leaning back and forth as you move. Keep your weight centered over the board, keep your head up, and use your arms for extra balance. One edge will dig into the snow, while the other edge lifts up. You will use edging to **carve**, or turn, down a hill.

The stomp pad is a rough mat located in front of the rear binding.

Notice how the toeside of the board is off the snow during a heelside edging.

14

Moving down a hill

Now you can try riding down a small hill. Choose a soft, short slope for your first run. With your back foot out of the binding, point your board down the slope and push off evenly. Put your back foot on the stomp pad and look ahead—not down. Keep most of your weight on your front foot.

As you first head downhill, concentrate on keeping your balance.

Both feet

After you make it to the bottom of the hill safely a few times, try strapping in both feet at the top of the hill. To get started, you must use your center of gravity again. Lean your hips down the hill. As long as you are near the edge of the slope, you will start to move.

As you start moving, bring your waist back over the center of the board. Crouch slightly and look ahead. If you wish, try pivoting to steer the board left or right. As you turn your lower body, keep your head facing downhill and watch where you are going.

Stop and go

Stopping is the second most important skill after learning to move. After all, you don't want to be like a runaway car on the hill! You may first learn to stop by accidentally falling on your backside, but the best way to stop is similar to the way hockey players stop when they are skating.

Dig in!

Imagine rolling a ball down the ski hill. It would roll in a straight line down the mountain. This straight line is often called the **fall line**. To stop, you need to turn your board against the fall line and dig your **uphill edge**, or edge that is closer to the top of the hill, into the snow. Most people find stopping easier if their heel edge is their uphill edge because their bodies face downhill as they stop. You can also make your toe edge the uphill edge, however.

Use your back foot to pivot the board quickly against the fall line. Dig your uphill edge hard into the snow. Lean toward the top of the hill and place your weight evenly on both feet. The harder you dig in, the faster you'll stop.

Traversing

Most hills are too steep to ride in a straight line. If you did, you would go so fast that you'd lose control. **Traversing** allows you to get downhill with control. To traverse, you basically slide back and forth on your board. Part of the time, you are riding backwards, or **fakie**. This movement might sound difficult, but start off on a bunny hill and you can master it quickly.

From regular to fakie

1. Start riding forward with your weight on the heel edge. Point your front foot slightly down the hill and point your arms to the left. You will move to the left.
2. Get ready to switch to fakie. Push your back foot forward so that it is a little farther down the hill than your front foot is. Switch your arms to your right side and lean to the right with your hips. You will move backward to the right.
3. As you start to gain speed going across the hill, stand up straighter but keep your arms out to the right.
4. When you reach the other side of the hill, bring your arms back across your body to the left and shift your front foot forward. Keep leaning back on the heel edge the whole time. Shift your hips to the left and ride forward again.

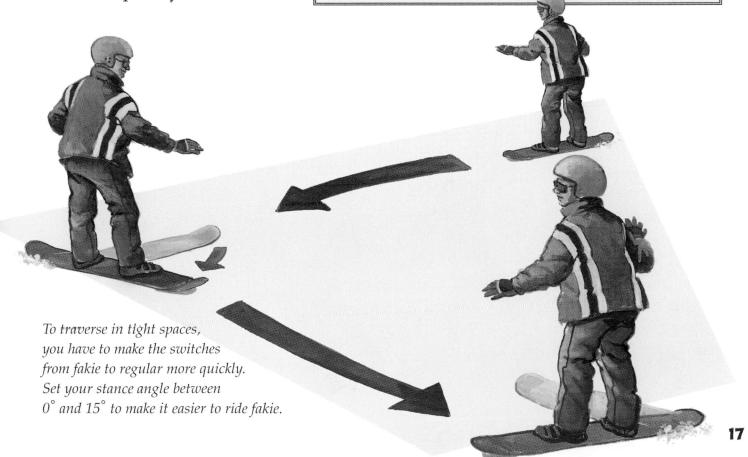

To traverse in tight spaces, you have to make the switches from fakie to regular more quickly. Set your stance angle between 0° and 15° to make it easier to ride fakie.

Turning

Turning allows snowboarders to do two things: control their speed and avoid obstacles such as trees, rocks, and other people. There are three types of turns. The most common are **skidded turns**, which use pivoting, and **carved turns**, which use edging and leaning to turn the board. The third type, **jump turns**, are done by making small hops and turning in midair.

Racers use hard carved turns to move quickly with control. The board is balanced right on the edge.

Note: If you find any techniques difficult, keep practicing. Don't be afraid to take extra time to learn something properly.

Skidded turns

These turns involve moving your back foot to push your board into a turn. To turn left, **skid**, or slide, your back foot out to the right. As your foot pushes out, lean your hips and waist to the left and into the turn. Allow your edge to dig into the snow. After the turn is complete, bring your body back into a more upright position.

Carved turns

Carved turns are more exact than skidded turns. They use the edges of the board. To carve, you must push your edges through the snow.

In a left turn, use your knees and ankles to push your heel edge down and lift your toe edge off the snow. It feels forced at first, but carving is the smoothest way to turn on a snowboard.

Left turn (heel edge)

Right turn (toe edge)

Make a chain

Snowboarders usually do **linked turns**, or turns that are done one after the other, as they ride the hill. Smooth linked turns give you the most control over your board. You can link both skidded and carved turns. To perform linked turns, begin turning in one direction. As soon as the turn is complete, start turning in the other direction. You can also adjust the size of the turns. Large sweeping turns are slow, whereas sharp short turns move you quickly down the mountain.

Getting a lift

Lifts are used to carry people up a hill. The most common lift is the **chair lift**. These long padded benches hang from a thick cable and carry between one and four people. If you are really lucky, one day you will ride the limousine of lifts—the **gondola**. Gondolas are fully-enclosed lifts that can hold six to ten people. They are used on extremely high slopes.

Tows pull people along the ground and up a hill. A few beginner runs use **rope tows**, a simple rope that you grab with your hands, but **t-bars** and **pomas** are more common tows. They have bars or discs that riders place between their legs. The most difficult part of using any lift, however, is getting on and off. Confidence and balance are the keys to safe lift riding.

Sitting down

The most common reason people have trouble getting on a chair lift is that they are scared. Don't be frightened! All you need to do is get into position and sit down.

1. Remove your rear foot from the binding before getting into the lift line. Slide through the line until it's your turn. Once the people ahead of you get in their chair, move into position. Stand with your back to the chair and your knees slightly bent. Look over your shoulder and watch your chair approach.

2. As soon as the chair meets the back of your knees, fall back onto it. Do not lean forward. Just let the chair sweep you off your feet. Then use one hand to grab the safety bar and bring it down into position.

Getting off

The key to getting off the lift is being ready. Prepare to get off as you get close to the unloading platform.

1. Raise the safety bar a few seconds before you reach the unloading platform. Slide yourself about an inch forward and point your board forward and slightly up. Place your back foot over the stomp pad so it does not slide off the board.

2. At the platform, use your hands to push yourself off the chair. Look straight ahead as you glide down the platform. Do not take your foot off the stomp pad until you stop. Use your arms to keep your balance.

Waiting in line

Boarders and skiers wait to ride the lift in a lift line. These lines can be short or long, depending on the time of day or the popularity of the runs around the lift. No matter how long the line is, move in an orderly fashion. Don't try to get ahead in the line. You may get your lift ticket taken away!

Powder and ice

On most ski runs, you will find an average amount of snow—not too much, not too little. Snow conditions can change from day to day, however. Sometimes fresh, heavy snow falls the night before you hit the slope. At other times, you'll find that machine-made snow is being used. Natural snow is much softer than machine-made snow, so each condition requires slightly different snowboarding skills.

Fluffy but heavy

Fresh, deep snow is called **powder**. Boarding in powder is a lot of fun, but you need to be careful. You never know how deep the snow is. In some places, you can find yourself up to your thighs in powder. If you go through powder too slowly, the soft snow will stop you completely. When approaching deep snow, get a lot of speed—don't worry about turning or edging. Powder can also hide rocks and other obstacles, so don't wander off the run.

Slippery surfaces

The "ice" that you find on a ski hill is usually not real ice, just very hard snow. It is often slightly shinier than normal snow. Even if you do not see the ice, you will feel it when you ride over it. Snowboards can slide out of control on ice, so you must use your edges like hockey skates to dig into it. Imagine pushing into the hill with your heel or toe edge and lean hard into it. Get to softer snow as soon as you can, so you can turn or stop.

As you enter the powder, do not let your snowboard dig into the snow, or it may get stuck. Lean toward the hill so that the board's nose or edge lifts off the snow.

23

Bumpy rides

Some difficult runs are covered with large bumps called moguls. When riding moguls, use your legs as giant springs. As you go up a mogul, curl your legs into your body. When you come down the mogul, push your legs down and stand tall. Remember to keep your eye on the moguls ahead so that you won't be surprised by larger bumps or other people.

Plan your jumps

If you get enough speed on moguls or other bumps, chances are you will leave the ground. Jumping is thrilling, but wiping out after a jump is not much fun. In fact, it hurts! If you plan your jumps before you try them, they will be safer and more successful. Never try a jump off a mogul unless there is a flat space for your landing.

Getting jumpy

Before jumping off a bump, be sure there are no people near where you will land. Build up some speed and hit the **lip**, or edge, of the bump straight on—do not be in the middle of a turn. As you hit the lip, you can also push off with your feet, but you don't have to. Once in the air, tuck your legs up into your body and keep your arms outstretched.

As you land, bring down both legs evenly so that your feet hit the ground at the same time. Bend your legs a bit to absorb the landing.

25

Freestyle

Freestyle snowboarding is popular and a lot of fun. Freestyle is closely related to skateboarding, sharing many of the same tricks. One of the first tricks you should learn is the **ollie**. The ollie is a way to jump up without using a ramp or bump. The ollie is a great trick on its own, and it is also used to perform many other moves.

Up and away

Ollies are great for freestyle snowboarding, but you can also use them in everyday riding to jump small obstacles such as rocks or large sticks.

1. Gain some speed and move in a straight line on the base of your board. Do not ride the edges. Bend your knees and crouch into a low position.

2. Lean back and quickly lift your front leg up and forward. Push hard off the ground with your back leg.

3. Bring your legs up. As you come down to land, allow your knees to bend to absorb the landing.

A nollie is similar to an ollie, but instead of pushing off the ground with your tail, you push off with your nose.

Expanding your tricks

Once you can do ollies and nollies, you can really begin to have fun with tricks. **Spins** and **straight airs** are two basic ways to expand your freestyle tricks. You do a spin by turning your board around. If you turn halfway around, it is a 180° spin. If you turn all the way around, it is a 360° turn. To make your tricks more complex, you can add a grab by holding a part of the board with one or both hands. A straight air is a jump in which you grab the board while making a turn that is under 360°. Depending on where you grab the board and which hand you use, the trick has different names.

Halfpipes

You can use ollies or moguls to get off the ground, but ramps will get you even more **air**, or height. The most impressive ramps are **halfpipes**. A halfpipe looks like a giant "U"—it has raised sides and a deep, wide valley in the middle. Snowboarders take turns dropping in at the entry ramp. They then perform tricks in the air at either side of the ramp. The tricks are usually based on spins and grabs. If boarders get enough air, they can include many spins and straight airs to make their tricks very complex. The best thing for a beginner, though, is to get a feel for the halfpipe.

Take it easy

When you first try a halfpipe, don't attempt anything too fancy. Start by dropping onto the ramp. As you drop in, bend your knees to keep your legs flexible. **Slide turns** are skidded turns done on the walls of the halfpipe. They are a simple way to ride the ramp. As you come up the wall, move your shoulders and head in the direction you wish to turn. Allow the rest of your body to follow and turn back down the ramp.

Remember, when traversing across the ramp, your uphill edge should be the one dug into the snow.

Getting some air

One of the biggest challenges of getting air is turning in midair. Start learning midair turns on a small, worn-out halfpipe. Approach the lip as though you were going to do a slide turn. Just as you reach the lip, do a quick jump. Turn in midair immediately by rotating your body. Look at the spot where you want to land to help you complete the turn. Absorb the landing with bent knees and continue riding. Did you land without falling? Congratulations! That small turn was a 360° aerial spin. As your confidence grows, you can try this spin on a larger halfpipe.

When you are in the air, look at the lip of the ramp. Your eyes will help lead your body to a safe landing.

Racing

Snowboard racing requires great skill. Even the smallest misstep can cost a race. Racers travel so fast that wearing helmets is essential. They also wear tight body suits to help their speed and hard boots to give them as much control as possible over the board.

Turn, turn, turn

Snowboard races are different lengths, but most are **slalom** races. In slalom races, riders must turn around posts called **gates**. If riders miss a gate, they may be disqualified. In normal slalom races, the gates are placed close together. The racers must turn often to get around each gate. Normal slalom courses are often fairly short, and the racers turn so much that they do not build up much speed.

Super G and **giant slalom** races are much faster. In these races, the gates are placed far apart so that the racers can gain a lot of speed between them. Falling in a giant slalom or super G race can cause serious injuries.

slalom

giant slalom

Racing day

Many ski hills have clubs that hold races. If you're interested, sign up! When your race day arrives, there are a few things to keep in mind. You may not be moving as fast as the pros, but wearing a helmet is still a good idea. If you can, get a look at the course before you ride it and try to remember any bumps or oddly placed gates that might give you trouble.

Boom!

Races are always close, so get a good start. Racers start in little booths with hand supports. As soon as you get the signal, use your arms to launch yourself onto the course. Once you have started, keep your upper body still and use your lower body to turn and absorb bumps.

Use carved turns when you race—skidding slows you down. Remember to start your turns before you reach the gate—your turn should be finishing just as you round the gate. As soon as you pass one gate, look ahead to the next one.

If you are one of the later racers, be alert for icy spots. With so many people turning on the same spot, the snow can get packed down.

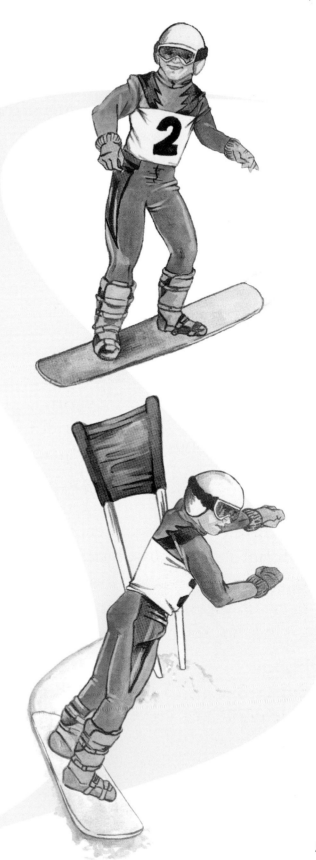

Glossary

Note: Boldfaced words defined in the book may not appear in the glossary

carve To turn on the snowboard's edge

course A marked track on which snowboarding races are held

extreme Describing snowboarding done on rough terrain; also called backcountry snowboarding

fakie Describing a method of snowboarding in which the snowboarder rides with the tail of the board leading

freestyle Describing snowboarding that involves jumps and tricks

halfpipe A deep, curved apparatus on which snowboarders perform tricks

hybrid Describing boots that combine the styles of hard boots and soft boots

lodge A rest building at a ski resort

slalom Describing a type of race in which snowboarders travel back and forth between gates as they travel down a hill

stance angle The position of the bindings on the snowboard, based on the boarder's comfort and the type of snowboarding for which the board will be used

unweight To reduce one's body weight on an edge in order to make a turn

weight To throw one's body weight onto an edge in order to make a turn

Index

1 2 3 4 5 6 7 8 9 0   Printed in the U.S.A.   1 0 9 8 7 6 5 4 3 2